weather
the wait

Volume II

30-day Devotional Journal for Women
Preparing for Their Kingdom Marriage Promise

JANAY WELLS

Published by Janay Wells

Editing and graphic design by Karen Bowlding

Cover Image by Moojoice

ISBN: 979-8-9855304-9-0

Acknowledgments

Dear God: Thank you for believing in me to write this book. Thank you for downloading to me each devotional. Thank you for continuing to give me strength and hope as I write. I know this will encourage every person who reads it. Thank you for trusting me with this assignment. Thank you for the vision and provision to complete this assignment. I know you will blow my mind! I thank you for every person this book reaches.

-

Dear Mom and Dad: Thank you for helping me with my business and guiding me in the right direction.

-

Dear Ms. Kerra: Thank you for believing in the *Weather the Wait* Ministry. Thank you for encouraging me as I write these devotionals. Thank you for spending countless hours on the phone pouring into me. Thank you for giving me guidance in my waiting process and being a true friend.

-

Dear Ms. Jackie, my spiritual mom: thank you for encouraging me throughout this experience. Thank you for holding me accountable to the Word of God. Thank you for speaking the Word over my life and reminding me of God's promises. Thank you for praying and interceding on my behalf and being there for me.

-

Dear Mr. Rich Christie, Jr., my spiritual father: thank you for being a great encouragement throughout this experience. Thank you for helping me to find Scriptures and understand the Bible better. Thank you for checking in and believing in me, even when I found it difficult to believe in myself.

-

Dear Ms. Sallie Eccles: Thank you for referring me to Ms. Karen for book consulting services. You have inspired me with your first book! Thank you for helping me with the process. I'm glad we have been able to share our poetry together.

-

Dear Ms. Karen: Thank you for helping me to work on the second volume of the *Weather the Wait* series. It looks amazing!

-

Dear Dr. Erica D. Montgomery: Thank you for mentoring me. Thank you for encouraging and pouring into me.

-

Dear Janelle Cumberbatch: I found you on YouTube and you have encouraged me so much in the waiting process. I have found your videos to bring warmth and comfort during my waiting/healing season. Thank you for being a part of my book! I pray that you will continuously uplift and encourage those that God puts in your path.

-

Dear Nadesha McPherson: Your videos on YouTube have brought so much confirmation to me during my waiting process. I love that the Lord speaks to you through different songs. Continue to be a prophetic voice helping those wait for the promises of the Lord to manifest. Thank you for being a part of my book! I know God is adding fuel to take you even higher than you can ask, think, or imagine!

-

Dear Jessica Dos Santos: Kingdom Influencer!!! Someone sent me a video of yours a couple years ago. I had already ran into your channel and found confirmation through your videos. You have encouraged me through the waiting process of kingdom marriage. You have created a mantle for those that are trying to remain in faith during their waiting season. Thank you for being a part of my book!

-

Dear YouTube family: Thank you for being on this journey with me! I'm so glad that God connected us to encourage one another. I know God is going to show off in your lives. I thank you for every like, kind comment, and share. You all continue to amaze me!

Dedication

"Blessed is she who has believed that the Lord would fulfill his promises to her!"

- Luke 1:45, NIV

I wrote the *Weather the Wait* series for those who have received a kingdom marriage promise from the Lord, struggle in their faith in the wait, may feel like there is no one for them, and strive to do God's will and seek purity through Him. To my YouTube family, friends, and anyone else that this book will encourage, it is dedicated to you. Continue to be steadfast in prayer and obedient to God's every instruction. Continue to hold onto faith, despite what you may be seeing. Believe in your kingdom marriage promise from God. Believe you can rest in God because He has His absolute best for you. Wait on Him and be patient. Go through the necessary processes. Watch how beautiful He will write your love story.

I Want To Be Chosen

I want to be chosen
I want to be the one he sees, I want him to see me like you see me

The one you have for me, he will surprise me and get down on one knee
He will know and hear your voice speaking, the one who is meant for me

I want to be chosen, I want to be pursued, I want to be found
Lord, you have already prepared his steps to find me

He will see my value, for you say a virtuous woman is hard to find for her price is above rubies
I want to be chosen

Preface

This book is part two of the Weather the Wait Series. Currently, I'm writing from my personal experiences, but also prophetically writing what God is wanting to say through me. I'm working on my master's degree in mental health counseling and working in mental healthcare. After I wrote the first book, I realized I was meeting a need.

Sometimes, when God shows us something and it doesn't look or feel like it's happening, it may feel like the opposite. Although you may have grown tired, weary, or started to get discouraged, act to restore your faith. Before I get married, I have more healing to do. More stuff needs to come out of me before I am one with my kingdom spouse. In the wait, there is a purpose. At 23, I'm accomplishing a lot. I'm working on my third book, the online Janay Wells Show, which is growing and reaching people over the world, and staying focused on my studies as God is preparing me to be a mental health counselor and eventually a psychologist when I earn a PhD.

At times, I have become frustrated and tired in the wait. I tend to be anxious and worry just about everything. The Lord is working on me. I felt frustration and anxiety, mainly for rushing the season or for expecting something to happen when it wasn't the appointed time. I learned to surrender my timelines, even after the Lord has shown something. Just because the Lord showed you something and you don't see it happening, it doesn't mean it won't come to pass. I learned to wait on the Lord, trust Him with what He shows me, to seek His face and presence, and truly rest. Rest must take place in the waiting process. This is just the beginning, and I'm preparing for what the Lord has for me. I know I will see it in due season. Whether we feel movement or not, in this season, there is purpose. God doesn't stop working. Heaven is busy orchestrating what the Lord is doing in your life.

Opening Prayer

Father God, I thank you for each person that will read this book. I pray you would speak directly to them through each devotional. Holy Spirit speak to their hearts what they need to know. May their hearts become uplifted, and they would have a sound mind in your presence. May your presence overwhelm the fears and doubts that surround them. May your peace that transcends all understanding guard their hearts and minds in Christ Jesus. May they learn to trust in you and wait for your every move. In Jesus' mighty name, amen.

Opening Encouragement

I started the *Weather the Wait Series* in an act of obedience and faith. This volume is like the first. By reading, you can build your faith muscles as you wait. Continue to seek God's face and His Will and not lean on your own understanding. Choose to be led by the Holy Spirit. Many have no idea who will be their spouse. Others may know who their spouse is and it's not time for pursuit. Some know who their spouse is and are in a committed relationship, moving towards marriage. Whatever phase you are in, faith and obedience are required to get to the next level. Once married, you will need faith and obedience during the storms you may have to weather with your spouse.

Continue to trust God, even when you don't see or feel anything moving. He is the answer to every question mark, every comma, and semicolon. When you don't know where to turn or what to do, He is there to lead us and guide us. We are weathering the wait together!

Stay Encouraged,
Janay Wells

Dear Future Husband

By Janay Wells

I have been praying for you.
I have been thinking about you.
I wonder if you know who I am.
I wonder if you can see me.
Are you ready for me?

Dear Future Husband
I have been waiting for you.
It seems long, but I know the preparation will be worth
it.
I have been trying to become the one, not just find the
one.

I have been through many broken hearts.
I'm hoping with you we will have a fresh start.
I'm trying not to bring the horse before the cart.
I can't wait for us to make beautiful music and art.
I know when we come together, we will never part.

Our faith is what will keep us together, I will never depart.

You will be my one and only, forever in my heart.

Table of Contents

Acknowledgements
Dedication
I Want To Be Chosen
Preface
Opening Prayer
Opening Encouragement
Dear Future Husband

I Give You My Heart 1

Heart Check 5

Record Keeper 10

Healer to the Broken-Hearted 14

Free Yourself 19

Pruning 24

The Fruits of the Spirit 28

Refined as Pure Gold 32

Rise and Shine 36

Seek the Kingdom of God 40

Write the Vision 44

A New Thing 49

Strength in the Process 53

Watch Your Mouth 57

Seeds of Faith 61

Faith Activated 67

Change Your Tune 72

Yes and Amen 76

Get out of God's Way 80

Tug of War in Faith... 86

Rise and Pray... 90

Kairos 94

Worth the Wait.. 98

Purpose Over Preference 103

Now You're Speaking My Language........................... 107

Love in Action... 112

Fill Me Up.. 117

Faith Over Fear... 122

Dancing Shoes 127

Full Circle 131

Closing Prayer
Closing Encouragement
Future Mrs. Poem
Exclusive Encouragement by Janelle
Exclusive Encouragement by Nadesha
Exclusive Encouragement by Kingdom Influencer
Reference
About the Author
Contact Page

I give you My Heart

"You will seek me and find me when you seek me
with all your heart."

- Jeremiah 29:13, NIV

I picked up a journal from a store where I used to work. A Scripture was on the cover. It was at a time when I didn't give God my whole heart. I thought I did, but I was still holding on to it. I projected my insecurities on to God. It wasn't fair. God is not man. We shouldn't expect Him to do what others have done to us. God is perfect; there is no flaw in Him. I based my responses to God on what men had done to me. I had a hard time trusting Him. Too many men easily walked out of my life. Because I was seeking validation from others, I didn't know my identity and value in God. I experienced and seen unfaithfulness. I had a hard time trusting God's faithfulness. At times, I felt like I wasn't enough for God, even though he calls me a *masterpiece*. I felt God would leave me, even though His word says that He would never leave me nor forsake me (Deuteronomy 31:6).

To seek wholeness from God, we must surrender our heart. God wants all of us. He doesn't only want a part of us. The amazing thing about God is that He is not intrusive. He will patiently wait until we're ready to give our all to Him. When we seek God with our heart, He is fully able to heal any brokenness that is within us.

Nugget of Wisdom (NOW)

Give God your heart. He's the best one to have it.

Activation

Listen to "Have my Heart" by Maverick City.

Reflect

What areas of your heart have you been withholding from God?

_____

_____

_____

_____

What areas have you been looking for instead of seeking God's face?

_____

_____

_____

_____

What parts of God do you want to find as you give Him your heart?

_____

_____

_____

_____

Pray

Father God, thank you for always being there for me. Thank you for not giving up on me. I give you my whole heart, withholding nothing from you. I ask that you cleanse my heart and remove anything that is not like you. I ask that you unharden my heart and give me a heart of flesh. I repent for the times I have projected the acts of man onto you. Heal me from insecurity and brokenness. I come to you with my heart open, ready to receive Your presence. In Jesus' mighty name, amen.

Heart Check

"Search me, God, and know my heart; test me and know my anxious thoughts…"

- Psalm 139:23, NIV

While growing up, I struggled with anxiety. I carried it into my adult life. I had a lot of anxious thoughts about being married. I knew it was a God-given desire and purpose He wants to fulfill. I struggled with my thoughts and the fear of the unknown. As God started to download additional information to me about my kingdom marriage, the more I ruminated about things. For some of us God, shows us events before it happens; possibly a part of the prophetic calling on your life. When I wanted to know something, God answered, whether I asked Him or not, just so that I could be prepared. I tended to want more details about when and how and went around the merry-go-round with God. I later understood that most of the anxious thoughts were from trying to figure everything out. My flesh had to die. I was getting in the way by trying to surrender and hold onto control at the same time—clashing with God.

We need a heart check with God. Analyze your fears and anxious thoughts and allow Him to do the same. Perform a fact check on each one. During my training to become a mental health counselor, they train us in what is known as cognitive-behavioral therapy (CBT). One of the exercises is to examine our core beliefs about a situation. We may operate in cognitive distortions. This is when we inaccurately think, and it's negatively based. Some jump to conclusions, catastrophize, which is assuming the worst will happen, or have black and white thinking, etc. Once we understand our underlying core beliefs, we are able to view it in the correct lens. By using this counseling technique, we can turn irrational beliefs into rational ones. An anxious thought or feeling may not be true. We shouldn't carry our anxious thoughts into our kingdom marriage. Permit God to uproot them so those don't continue to grow.

now

It's time for a heart check from God.

Activation

Ask God to check your heart. Prepare to write down what He shows you.

Reflect

What did God find when he searched your heart?

_____

_____

_____

_____

What anxious thoughts are you experiencing or have experienced regarding your kingdom marriage?

_____

_____

_____

_____

In what ways has the Lord tested you? In what ways is He allowing your faith to become stronger?

_____

_____

_____

_____

_____

_____

_____

_____

Pray

Father God, I ask you check my heart and remove anything that's not like you. Remove any anxious thoughts I may have regarding my kingdom marriage promise. Purify me and renew the right spirit in me. Remove these same feelings my future spouse may be feeling. Heal me of anything that could be keeping from moving forward. Continue to cover me and my future spouse. Muzzle the mouth of the enemy that comes to speak anxiety and fear. Thank you in advance for moving on my behalf and my future spouse. Continue to cover us from harm, seen and unseen. Continue to cleanse my heart and increase the fruits of the spirit in me. In Jesus' mighty name, amen.

Day 3

Record Keeper

"You keep track of all my sorrows. You have collected all my tears in your bottle. You have recorded each one in your book."

- Psalm 56:8, NLT

Many times, I cried and didn't understand what was going on with my relationships with people. While growing up, my home environment was emotional and tumultuous. I often wondered where God was during the times when difficult events were taking place. When I think about the Scripture above, I see how God was detailed. During everything, He recorded each tear and sorrow. He must have a lot of jars of tears recorded for me in Heaven. He has so much joy for us than our sorrows, which is good news. Each one is accounted for and logged in His book, and He has provided a way for us to flourish. God is precise. He knows our thoughts before we do. He knows the number of hairs on top of our head. He is attuned with everything little thing that concerns us.

When we feel despair and want to cry, let it out. Someone may have broken our heart, left, or betrayed us. God is keeping count. He weeps with us. God doesn't take pleasure in our sadness. He comes to comfort us when we need it the most. On your journey to kingdom marriage, God is keeping record of everything.

now

God has recorded everything in His book.

Reflect

What are you feeling sorrowful for or crying about?

_____

_____

_____

_____

What events has the Lord carried you through?

_____

_____

_____

_____

What events do you look forward to on your journey to kingdom marriage?

_____

_____

_____

_____

Pray

Father God, thank you for being the record-keeper in my life. Thank you for recording my sorrows in your book, for being the promise keeper in my life, and uplifting me when I'm down. Thank you for continuing to encourage me in the promise you have for me. Thank you for strengthening me when I feel weary in the wait, restoring and renewing me in the process, and carrying me throughout. Thank you for covering my future spouse, protecting him from harm seen and not seen, and restoring his hope and joy. I thank you for continuing to connect the dots as we continue to wait on you and your perfect timing. I give you all the praise, honor, and glory. In Jesus' mighty name, amen.

Day 4

Healer to the Broken-Hearted

"The Lord is close to the brokenhearted and saves those who are crushed in spirit."

- Psalms 34:18, NIV

I don't have a positive feeling when I look back on my romantic relationships. I was in several short-term relationships. I was the one who cared more. I had low self-esteem. I kept picking the same type of guys; those that didn't want long-term commitment. At our age, I understood, but I felt used and sometimes abused. Because of my codependency, I allowed certain men to come back into my life. Most of them, if not all of them, just wanted to have the benefits of a relationship without being committed. One benefit is now on reserve for my future husband. Why did I allow those men to use me, to get what they wanted, and leave? Something was broken in me. I must have thought it is what I was worth. I wasn't worth a long-term commitment. I wasn't worth someone who just wanted to be with me. I had a list of insecurities. In one relationship, the guy liked half-naked women in front of me on a popular social media app. His excuse was that they were models. Every time he scrolled, there were more and more half-naked women that weren't models. I was hurt because he didn't regard my emotions. I wondered if I was enough. Would he have cheated if he had the opportunity? Was that what he wanted from me? Because of his actions, I became more insecure. He eventually unfollowed over 100 inappropriate accounts. It wasn't about me. He was dealing with lust.

Many times, I didn't want to be bothered with men. I just wanted to focus on my goals and play with my dog. At least my dog Sasha was loyal. She was there for me and wasn't going to leave like some of the men in my life. I questioned what was wrong with me. Occasionally, it was more about how I let others treat me. God was close to me every time my heart was broken. I felt God's arms wrap around me. I was crushed, hurt, and felt alone. God was there to remind me each time of His love for me.

No matter how your heart was broken, God will not leave you. God is always faithful, even when we are not always faithful to Him. The man of God He has for you will encourage you. He won't be perfect, but neither are you. The important thing is to be whole in God. He already knows when your heart breaks. In His perfect love, He comes and puts the broken pieces together and makes it whole again.

now

You will not be two halves coming together, but two wholes coming together.

Activation

If you're currently going through a heartbreak or disappointment, ask God how He is healing it.

Reflect

Are you currently going through a heartbreak or disappointment?

_____

_____

_____

_____

What heartbreaks have you gone through and how has God restored you from those disappointments?

_____

_____

_____

_____

In what ways do you think you will appreciate your future husband because of those disappointments and hurts?

_____

_____

_____

_____

Pray

Father God, thank you for healing my heart time and time again, binding up my heart each time it was broken, and restoring my heart and allowing me to feel whole again. I thank you for what the enemy meant for my harm; you will turn it around for my good. I thank you for the broken-hearted moment because I will be able to appreciate my future spouse more. Thank you that my kingdom marriage promise is coming. I thank you for the joy and peace it will add to my life. I pray over my future husband's heart. I ask that you make it whole. I pray that every disappointment and heartbreak would be mended. I thank you for restoring his heart as well. I will continue to trust in you with my whole heart and lean not on my own understanding. I will continue to acknowledge you in all my ways, and I know you will make my paths straight. In Jesus' mighty name, amen.

Day 5

Free Yourself

"Therefore confess your sins to each other and pray for each other so that you may be healed. The prayer of a righteous person is powerful and effective."

- James 5:16, NIV

One time, while being in the presence of God, He told me that I needed to forgive to move forward. I thought I forgave those who hurt me or broke my heart. If God was bringing it to my attention, I still hadn't fully forgiven those people. I wanted to be made whole. I wanted to no longer be in bondage. I didn't want to stay in any unforgiveness, and I didn't want it to hold up what God was trying to do. I started talking with Ms. Jackie and Ms. Kerra. I told them what I was struggling with. They hold me accountable to God's Word and help me to effectively pray.

By forgiving others, we can free ourselves. We must not harbor resentment and hurt. God knows what we have endured, and He will vindicate us. As often said, "Unforgiveness is like drinking poison and expecting the other person to die." This analogy is used to express how holding onto anger and unforgiveness only harms us. It only keeps us in bondage, meanwhile the other person is going on living their life. Many times, God is wanting to bring our kingdom marriage, but we aren't fully healed. God wants to get all the glory. It won't be to prove someone wrong. It won't be out of pride. It will be for God to get the credit. We must continue to release anything that isn't of God. Despite what we see, we must trust Him in the process. We must stand in righteousness and continue to pray according to His will for our lives.

now

Forgiveness is for yourself.

Activation

Talk with God about all unforgiveness you're retaining and what you need to confess. Say aloud the people or situations you need to forgive. Repent for your transgressions. Father God, I come to you, and I repent for harboring unforgiveness. I forgive

(say person or situation), and I release it to you.
In Jesus' mighty name, amen.

Reflect

What sins have you confessed to Godly counsel?

_____

_____

_____

_____

Are you holding on to any unforgiveness? What or who do you need to forgive?

_____

_____

_____

_____

In what ways are you being healed or have been healed? What is God trying to teach you in this season?

_____

_____

Pray

Father God, I thank you that you have paid the ultimate price. I thank you that I no longer have to be in bondage. I release all unforgiveness and confess and repent of my sins to you. I ask that you make me whole. I ask that you continue to heal every broken part of me. I ask you to heal anything that is broken in my future husband. Thank you for surrounding me with the right people and connections. Thank you for removing the hindrances and delivering me from myself. I thank you that I'm healed, delivered, and set free. In Jesus's name, amen.

Day 6

Pruning

"He cuts off every branch in me that bears no fruit, while every branch that does bear fruit he prunes so that it will be even more fruitful."

- John 15:2, NIV

When I was going through the pruning stage, all I could say was, "Ouch." No one likes to go through a process when things and people are stripped from them. God was removing certain people from my life. He told me to discontinue a relationship. Other times, some people in my life went another way. I was alone at times, frustrated with the process, and didn't understand what and why certain events were taking place. I didn't realize why some people had to go until later. Now, I'm thankful God pruned those relationships from me. "Not everybody can go with you," is an often-used phrase. They weren't bad people. They just couldn't come with me to where God was sending me. God had to prune mindsets and attitudes before I entered a kingdom marriage. God was pruning my insecurities and things that didn't bear good fruit in my life. Some people weren't adding to my life, only taking away from me.

God desires us to be more fruitful. We may not understand at the time why we must remove certain people, things, or ways of thinking. We must learn to be obedient to what He is asking us to do. We must first trust God during the process of preparation. God doesn't just see us for where we've been or where we are now. He sees us for where we are going. Continue to let His process do a good work in you.

now

Allow God to remove the dead things off so that you can thrive.

Activation

Ask God what He needs to prune. Give God permission to access and remove those things that are no longer bearing good fruit. Write out those things.

Reflect

What is God pruning or has pruned?

_____

_____

_____

_____

What are some things that God wants to add or restore in you?

_____

_____

_____

_____

What are some ways you can trust God more during the pruning process?

_____

_____

_____

_____

Pray

Father God, thank you for removing everything that is dead and doesn't bear good fruit. Thank you for pruning me and allowing what is fruitful to continue to grow in my life. Remove mindsets, attitudes, and habits that are not of you. Disconnect people that are hindering me and replace with those that will help me along my way. Thank you for going before me and making my paths straight. Thank you for canceling the assignment of the enemy over my life. I thank you that all things will work together for my good. I thank you that you will use these things and turn them around for my good. In Jesus's mighty name, amen.

Day 1

The Fruits of the Spirit

"But the fruit of the Spirit is love, joy, peace, patience, kindness, goodness, faithfulness, gentleness, self-control..."

-Galatians 5:22-23, ESV

I will go through seasons when the Lord tests fruits in me. One season, God grows patience in me, and in another, it's self-control. Normally, we can see what fruit He is growing by what's happening around us. When I started my purity journey, God was growing in me patience, goodness, and self-control. God was trying to increase some things in me, but I first had to decrease. God may be trying to grow in you patience and long suffering in the wait. God may be trying to increase your peace and faithfulness in Him as you wait. God may even be examining your attitude in the wait. Is it loving, joyful, gentle, and kind? Sometimes, we may have to wait longer than anticipated because God needs certain fruits to be more evident in our life. At times, I laugh with God because there are things He is growing in me before I get married. Patience is a fruit I struggle with because I want to be in control of how everything is going to work out. This doesn't require faith.

God is not on our time. He is outside of time. He isn't going to move any faster because we want Him to. God needs to grow these fruits in us first. If He doesn't, the man can come along and we may not be patient, loving, gentle, or kind to him. That man may turn around and walk the other direction. Rest in knowing what God is doing in you in this season of your life.

now

Be fruitful and let it overflow into the lives of others.

Activation

Ask God what fruits you've developed and what fruits you still need to work on.

Reflect

What fruits are strong in you? Explain.

_____

_____

_____

_____

What fruits are God trying to grow in you before your kingdom marriage?

_____

_____

_____

_____

What ways does God want you to be more fruitful in the spirit?

_____

_____

_____

_____

Pray

Father God, I thank you for seeing me for who I am and all that you have called me to be. Help me to become more fruitful in the spirit. Help me to be more patient while waiting for my kingdom marriage. Help me to be kind to people even when they're not kind to me. Help me to have peace in this situation when something doesn't look certain. Help me to continue to be faithful in what you have asked of me. Help me to be gentle in my words and actions against others and to myself. Help me to continue to be righteous in your eyes and to practice goodness in your presence. Help me to have self-control over my struggles. God, you know what fruits I need to grow. Help to cultivate and grow these fruits of the spirit in my life. Continue to guide where you are leading me. Help me to display your character through every storm and season. In Jesus' mighty name, amen.

Day 8

Refined as Pure Gold

"But he knows the way that I take; when he has tested
me, I will come forth as gold."

- Job 23:10, NIV

God is refining me before my kingdom marriage. He is removing impurities and preparing me as I wait. God has tested me through the waiting period to see if I would wait and be obedient. It didn't feel good while God was purifying me. I had many insecurities and mindsets that needed to be removed before my kingdom marriage. God allows tests of our faith to stretch us and to continue to stand on His Word. We must go through the fire to become gold. We must go through the process no matter how uncomfortable it may get. God knows exactly what needs to be purified in us. Pure gold is made by reaching its melting point. The impurities rise to the top in a separate layer. Once removed, it has been refined and becomes pure gold.

God is allowing our impurities to rise to the surface so that He can remove them. Purification is not easy, but it's necessary before your kingdom marriage. We need to allow God to do the work in us so that we don't have to keep being tested in the same area. We don't want to keep going through that fiery process again and again. God will allow us to keep being retested until we learn what He is trying to do. God knows what direction we want to go in and what we want to do. God is going to test us, but the end result will be pure gold.

now

"It's not over til it's gold."

- Dr. Neisha-Ann Thompson

Activation

Write a list of impurities that God is trying to refine out of you.

Reflect

Has God been refining you and removing impurities before your marriage? If so, what things is He removing or have removed?

_____

_____

_____

_____

What is God replacing in you as He is removing your impurities?

_____

_____

_____

_____

What is it that God is requiring of you in this season of refinement? What changes are you willing to make?

_____

_____

_____

_____

Pray

Father God, thank you for removing my impurities. Thank you for testing me so that I may come out as pure gold. Continue to renew and refine me. Anything that is not pleasing to you, take it out and replace it with your Holy Spirit. Refine ways that I have that aren't going to work when I get married. Teach me your ways and how to better respond while I'm going through a process that isn't easy. Give me the words to speak when I'm going through a season when I'm being tested. Continue to refine my future husband. Remove anything from him that isn't like you. Continue to bless and favor him in the midst of it all. I ask that you lead and guide him where he needs to be. I pray for Godly accountability as we go through the purification process. Heal any areas that still require healing. Deliver us from everything we are bound to. In Jesus' mighty name, amen.

Day 9

Rise and Shine

"Arise, shine, for your light has come, and the glory of the Lord rises upon you."

- Isaiah 60:1, NIV

I started to get weary from getting up every day and completing the assignments in front of me while going to school studying mental health counseling and preparing for my business and show. I was excited to continue what the Lord had called me to do. I knew it was for a purpose and for God to get the glory. Being a light in the darkness isn't easy. I faced opposition from people and the enemy. I knew I had to push past the oppression and opposition and continue to be a beacon of light. I knew God was sustaining me each day.

I encourage you to rise and shine! Continue to get up and do what the Lord has asked you to do. Despite how you feel, keep pressing because the glory of God is upon you. Do it afraid. Do it when no one is looking. Do it even when you don't have all the details. God has called you to be a light at your school, on your job, and maybe on a social media platform. Your kingdom marriage is going to shine a light and the glory of God will be evident in your marriage. Your kingdom marriage will have a specific mission of how you will bring people into the kingdom of God. Continue to rise above barriers. Continue to rise above the thoughts and feelings of inadequacy. You have been called by the Most High.

now

Girl, get up. God's got this!

Activation

Accomplish something today that God is asking you to do.

Reflect

What is the Lord asking you to work on in this season?

_____

_____

_____

_____

How are you being a light before your kingdom marriage?

_____

_____

_____

_____

Have you been experiencing any setbacks and opposition?
If so, how are you pressing through?

_____

_____

_____

_____

Pray

Father God, thank you for calling me and seeing me. Thank you for the assignments you have given me this season. Thank you for giving me the proper grace through each assignment. Help me to continue to be a light in the darkness. Help me not to become weary in well doing. I pray over my future spouse and ask that you cover him. Continue to bless the work of his hands. May he not grow weary in well doing. I thank you for our kingdom marriage that will be coming together. I thank you for the purpose and glory that will be displayed in our marriage. In Jesus' mighty name, amen.

Day 10

Seek the Kingdom of God

"But seek first the kingdom of God and his righteousness, and all these things will be added to you."

- Matthew 6:33, ESV

As my walk with God grew, I realized that God wants to be first in everything. He doesn't want our leftovers; He wants our best given to Him first. I desired to be in alignment with God in every area of my life. As the desire for marriage grew in my heart, I understood that God wanted to add something to me. I must submit to Him and seek His kingdom.

God is establishing an order. He says, "Seek me and all other needs will be added to you." Many times, we can get things out of order. When we seek God, we have security knowing that God has us. Many kingdom marriages will influence other people and bring purpose to what God is doing. God's purpose and glory should be displayed in your kingdom marriage. As we prepare and go through the process, we must continuously seek after God. We must be obedient to God about who we are to be with, where we ought to live, and the job we are to accept. If we want God's will, we must first be willing to submit and obey God's every instruction. Many of us are working on our individual kingdom assignments. This is important before marriage. We must be willing to complete what God has for us now, before He gives us a dual assignment with our husband.

now

Your kingdom marriage will be added to you once you seek the kingdom of God.

Activation

Have a conversation with God. What should you be seeking Him about? What are the things He wants to add to you?

Reflect

Have you been seeking God about everything? If not, what has stopped you from giving everything to him?

_____

_____

_____

_____

What individual assignments has the Lord given you to complete before your kingdom marriage?

_____

_____

_____

_____

What is God saying that He will add on to you?

_____

_____

_____

_____

Pray

Father God, I thank you for believing in me and entrusting me with my assignments. As I continue to seek you, I know everything else you have for me will be added on. I repent for the times that I didn't go to you first and when I wasn't obedient in what you have asked of me. I will continue to seek your will for my life. I thank you for my kingdom marriage promise. I thank you that in due season you will add that onto me. I thank you for giving me what I now need to accomplish what is required of me. I thank you that your grace is sufficient for me. I thank you for helping me along in this journey. I pray that I will continue to seek your kingdom. I understand I must decrease, and you must increase. I thank you for what you're doing in my future husband's life right now. I thank you that you are directing and covering him. I thank you that you are answering our prayers. I give you all the honor, glory, and praise. In Jesus' mighty name, amen.

Day 11

Write the Vision

"Write the vision; make it plain on tablets, so he may run who reads it. For still the vision awaits its appointed time; it hastens to the end—it will not lie. If it seems slow, wait for it; it will surely come; it will not delay."

- Habakkuk 2-3, ESV

As God was continuing to download to me, I kept notes. God gave me visions and dreams. A few years ago, I was hoping my future husband could sing or play a musical instrument. I wanted us to worship God together. It was just a thought or hope. It wasn't something I was thinking about too much. When I was young, I often wrote songs and sang. I wanted to have someone to be able to share my passions with. I had a dream and God showed me that my future husband would be gifted in this area.

Sometimes you can have a desire but may not be sure if it's God's will or just a desire.

In 2020, Ms. Kerra, a dear friend who is prophetic said to me, "He's very musical and creative."

I hadn't told her anything that God showed me at that time. I knew it was just more than a hope or a wish, but it would be a part of my kingdom marriage—we would make music together and worship God in spirit and in truth. I felt what Kerra said was confirmation. I also wanted someone who could build my talk show with me.

The spouse God has for you will add to and compliment you in areas. You will do the same for him. God has a purpose for both of you in your kingdom marriage. Hopes and wishes you may have forgotten about will be fulfilled. Kingdom-based marriages will influence others. Spouses in kingdom marriages will build the community and fulfill other purposes. Those that see it will be able to run with the vision. Although it awaits an appointed time or seems like it's taking too long, keep pressing. It will not delay at the end! Keep recording the visions God has shown you and keep believing that it will come to pass. Don't overlook the hints and clues God has given to you as a part of the greater vision.

now

The vision and purpose are bigger than just
the kingdom marriage.

Activation

Pray and ask God what the vision is for your kingdom marriage. Write it out in a notebook.

Reflect

What are things that your kingdom marriage will do to build the kingdom of God?

_____

_____

_____

_____

What support or help will you need? Who else will be running with the vision?

_____

_____

_____

_____

How will God help you wait for the vision to come to pass when it seems to be delayed?

_____

_____

_____

_____

Pray

Father God, thank you for giving me visions and your intentions. Thank you for sharing with me the secrets of Heaven. Help me to not get weary in well doing as I wait on your marriage promise. Thank you that no good thing shall you withhold. Help me to prepare for the vision and to make it plain so that others may see it and run with it. Give me the resources I need to build the kingdom according to your will and purpose. Help me to be receptive to what you need of me in this season. Help me to effectively pray as I write the vision and wait on the manifestations. I pray over my future husband's visions and that you will help him to flourish. I pray over our joint kingdom assignment and that there will be no hindrances. Give him patience as he is waiting on you. Bless the work of his hands in his season of building and preparing. Give him a finisher's anointing for the assignments he may have a hard time completing. Help us to not get frustrated when we don't see the vision taking place. Help us to wait for the appointed time, because in the end it shall not delay. In Jesus' mighty name, amen.

Day 12

A New Thing

"See, I am doing a new thing! Now it springs up; do you not perceive it? I am making a way in the wilderness and streams in the wasteland."

- Isaiah 43:19, NIV

As a young woman, I was going through the same relationship cycles regarding patterns and sin. As I truly surrendered myself to the Lord, God wanted to do a new thing in me. I didn't want what I kept receiving. I prayed, "God I want something new and something that will last." As I continued the journey with God, He was restoring me. After I started my purity journey a couple of years ago, God was saying, "I want to do something new in you." It didn't matter what my past was, God wanted to give me a fresh start. He wanted to renew something in me. He wanted to bless me with a relationship that would emulate His love. He wanted to make me whole so that my next relationship could be whole. God wants to develop a kingdom marriage for me and wants it to be different. He doesn't want it to be like everything else I've experienced.

Many times, we can be afraid of the new thing. We may keep ourselves in familiar cycles instead of stepping into the newness of what God is trying to do. God wants to do a new thing in our life. Sometimes we don't perceive it. The new thing may be in front of us, and we may not recognize it. God is making a way in the places that seem deserted and would not be fruitful. God is doing a new thing as we are preparing for our kingdom marriage. Allow God to renew you as you approach your kingdom marriage.

now

This time it's going to be different.

Activation

Ask God what newness He wants to do as you approach your kingdom marriage.

Reflect

What newness is God doing before your kingdom marriage? How is He preparing you?

_____

_____

_____

_____

What will be some differences that God is making or will make in your kingdom marriage promise compared to what you have experienced?

_____

_____

_____

_____

What areas in your life are dry and feel like a desert? How is God making provision in this season?

_____

_____

_____

_____

Pray

Father God, I thank you for doing a new thing in my life. Thank you that my upcoming kingdom marriage will be like nothing I've experienced. Thank you for connecting me to my future spouse and we shall come together and move forward as you see fit in your timing. Thank you for accounting for the hurts and disappointments. Thank you that this kingdom marriage is set up by you and will have your blessing on it. Thank you for covering us. Thank you for continuing to direct our paths. Help us to perceive what you're doing in this season, Lord. Help us to not miss what you're wanting us to see. Give us clarity to continue to walk the path you have set before us. When weariness sets in, help us to remember the promises you have spoken over our lives. Help us to continue to speak those things we don't see. Help us to not get frustrated when going through the process. Our faith must come up higher and we thank you that it's already done. In Jesus's name, amen.

Day 13

Strength in the Process

"Do not grieve, for the joy of the Lord is your strength."

- Nehemiah 8:10, NIV

As a young woman, I didn't always make the best relationship choices. I used to beat myself up for staying in unhealthy, even toxic relationships. I didn't know my worth and was codependent as if my worth was tied to it. I have been single for about two years and chosen not to date. I will continue to heal and focus on what God desires of me in this season.

For some of you, you may be experiencing a break-up, loss, or feel like there is no one for you. It's easy to grieve and stay in a place of defeat. However, God is strengthening you during the process. You may feel like you need more strength, but what you need is more of God's joy. You might not understand when someone is no longer in your life. You must trust God in the middle. When we aren't sure where to turn, we must depend on the Lord for His power. God is our strength when we feel weak. God knows what you need and the right time to give it to you. Believe that God is going to give you back so much more than you lost. Keep your hope and faith in the Lord, your kingdom marriage is coming.

now

Fresh joy is coming your way!

Activation

Talk with God. Write what has been stealing your joy.

Reflect

What has been stealing your joy in the waiting period?

_____

_____

_____

_____

What emotions have you been feeling in the waiting period?

_____

_____

_____

_____

How is God restoring your joy and strengthening you in the waiting season?

_____

_____

_____

_____

Pray

Father God, I thank you for giving me strength in the process. Thank you for renewing my strength and removing weariness. Thank you for continuing to lead and guide me through this process. Thank you that everything will work out for my good. Thank you for strengthening my future husband as well. Thank you for giving him the grace and strength he needs during this time. Thank you for teaching me what I need to learn in this season. In Jesus' mighty name, amen.

Watch your Mouth

"The tongue has the power of life and death, and those who love it will eat its fruit."

- Proverbs 18:21, NIV

Out of impatience and frustration, I have spoken out of place. I repented and renounced those things I said. We can get frustrated for many reasons and may want to speak how we feel, however, as intercessors, our words carry weight in the spiritual realm. We must be careful what we choose to speak. The enemy loves when we give him legal access. Don't do this! I encourage you to write in your journal about your feelings and talk with God.

In our kingdom marriage we will display God's purpose and glory on the Earth. According to our declarations and decrees, the atmosphere shifts. We must stand firm on what God told us. We must continue to pray in our heavenly language. The enemy doesn't understand what we are speaking to God. We are uttering mysteries to God. When I don't know what to pray about, the Spirit intercedes for me. If you don't have your heavenly language, ask God for the baptism of the Holy Spirit with the evidence of speaking in tongues. It may not happen right away. After I got filled, I mainly spoke in tongues when dreaming. I blocked the flow of doing it while awake because I overanalyzed it. I had to relax, decrease, and let it happen.

It eventually fully manifested, and now I speak in my heavenly language every day. Don't speak what you don't want to happen out of your mouth. Continue to talk with the Lord and speak life. Meditate on His word daily for strength and guidance.

now

If you don't want it to manifest, don't speak it
out of your mouth.

Activation

Repent and renounce everything negative word you
spoke over your kingdom marriage.

Reflect

Is there anything that you have spoken negatively about your future kingdom marriage? If so, what?

_____

_____

_____

_____

How can you speak life over your future kingdom marriage? What would you say?

_____

_____

_____

_____

What lessons have you learned from speaking over your future kingdom marriage? What would you do differently moving forward?

_____

_____

_____

_____

Pray

Father God, I repent and renounce the negative things I said about my kingdom marriage promise. Help me when I become frustrated. Help me when my faith becomes tired and I'm not seeing the full manifestations. I speak life over my kingdom marriage promise. I speak of healing, restoration, and deliverance. Thank you for making us whole. I declare and decree that my marriage will be blessed, that we will be able to withstand the tests and trials. My marriage will stand on the foundation and representation of Christ and the church. My marriage will be full of joy, love, and laughter. I pray for the times that may come to shake us, and even in those moments, I will still speak life and stand on God's word. In Jesus' mighty name, amen.

Seeds of Faith

He replied, "Because you have so little faith. Truly I tell you, if you have faith as small as a mustard seed, you can say to this mountain, 'Move from here to there,' and it will move. Nothing will be impossible for you."

- Matthew 17:20, NIV

As I prepare for my kingdom marriage, I often struggle in my faith. I'm not sure how God is going to put it together, but I have faith He will. I was planting seeds of faith. I prayed over myself, my future husband, and my online video community. I planted seeds of faith with each prayer and completed the assignment. I don't know the impact I will have through my obedience of planting these seeds.

It takes faith as small as a mustard seed. Elizabeth Elliot once said, "Don't dig up in doubt what you planted in faith." During the process, we may start to dig up when in doubt. You may cry out, "God, you have shown me this, but I don't see it happening. God, you asked me to stay in this place and I don't see any movement. God, you asked me to keep praying for this person and it seems like the opposite of what you said is happening. God, you told me to move to this place and it feels like I'm all alone."

Be careful with those you talk with about your kingdom marriage. Some will not have the faith to believe like you do. Others will discourage you, causing you to move out of the place of your obedience and faith. Despite what you see, keep sowing and believing. When you plant a seed, you bury it within the dirt and patiently wait for it to grow. The seed takes root, and you see something sprout from the ground, despite waiting for a long time. The environment matters. A seed needs the right amount of sunlight and water, not too much or too little. We must make sure we are in the right environment for our faith to continue to grow. We must make sure we are digging into the word of God, talking with God, and being in a community where our faith can grow. Overtime, we will see the full manifestations of the seeds of faith we have planted.

now

Keep sowing seeds of faith. You will soon have a harvest!

Activation

Praise God for what He has done. Praise Him for your kingdom marriage. Pray for His Will to be done on Earth as it is in Heaven.

Reflect

What seeds of faith have you been planting? How have you been cultivating these seeds?

_____

_____

_____

_____

What seeds of faith have others planted in you? What seeds have you planted in others?

_____

_____

_____

_____

What seeds of doubt and fear have you planted that must be uprooted?

_____

_____

_____

_____

How is God increasing your faith in this season?

_____

_____

_____

_____

Pray

Father God, I thank you for having faith in me even when I don't have faith in myself. Thank you for believing and hoping the best for me. I thank you for the seeds of faith others have planted in me. I know that it's impossible to please you without faith. I thank you God for adjusting the atmosphere according to my faith. I repent and renounce words I have spoken when I lacked faith. I repent for speaking what I see instead of walking in faith. I speak crop failure over the words I planted when I was in doubt and fear. Thank you for uprooting those negative seeds and preventing them from growing. Thank you in advance for my kingdom marriage. Thank you that my future marriage is blessed. Thank you that my future family is blessed. Thank you for working all things out according to your purpose. Thank you for getting me back into alignment when I go off course. Thank you that I won't lean on my own understanding in this season. Thank you that everything you have spoken over my life shall go forth and do what it has been sent to accomplish. I prophecy over every area of my life that it shall be aligned with the kingdom of God and your purpose for my life. I cancel out the assignment of the enemy over my kingdom marriage.

I take authority over every spirit that may come to steal, kill, and destroy the faith you have placed inside of me. I ask that anything that is not of you to break it off. In Jesus' mighty name, amen.

Day 16

Faith Activated

"So then faith *comes* by hearing, and hearing by the word of God."

- Romans 10:17, NKJV

One day, while scrolling through an online video website, I ended up on a prophetic video. It was my first time watching something like it. To some extent, I knew what it was and often heard the term prophesy at church but didn't know too much about it. Many of the prophetic voices I listened to were helpful in activating my faith. Many times, it was exactly what I needed to hear. The speaker perfectly aligned it to my situation. I took it back to the Lord and discussed with God what I heard.

After hearing the Word of God and listening to encouragement from church, online, through Ms. Kerra and Ms. Jackie, and others, I was able to reactivate my faith. In the beginning, I felt alone, because I wasn't in a community with people who were experiencing the same thing. After explanation from others and the prophetic words spoken over my life, I began to understand. I created a prophetic diary. In it I wrote about the dreams and visions God showed me. Later, I posted my prophetic word videos to encourage others. I wanted to use my experience to help others.

In this season, continue to activate your faith. Stay in God's Word and listen to encouraging messages. Your faith will move the hand of God. Be steadfast in your position of faith. Despite what you see, don't waver in your faith.

now

Faith is like a muscle. Keep exercising and activating your faith!

Activation

My faith is strong. My faith is activated. My faith is unshakeable and immovable. I will speak faith over my kingdom marriage. I won't just be a hearer of the word, but a doer of the word. My faith is planted from the foundation of your word and what you have spoken over me.

Reflect

How are you activating your faith in this season? What has been helping you to increase your faith?

_____

_____

_____

_____

In what ways has the enemy come to steal, kill, and destroy your faith in this season?

_____

_____

_____

_____

What Scriptures have you used to help you in your faith regarding your kingdom marriage promise?

_____

_____

_____

_____

How have other people helped you to activate your faith regarding your kingdom marriage promise?

_____

_____

_____

_____

Pray

Father God, thank you for helping me to activate my faith in you for my kingdom marriage promise. Thank you for removing fear or doubt. Thank you for canceling the enemy's assignment to steal, kill, and destroy my faith. Thank you for sending people my way to help build my faith. Thank you for increasing my future husband's faith. May he continue to seek your face and to rely on you. May he not get weary in well doing and frustrated. May we both walk by faith and not by sight. Help us in the unclear areas. Help up in those places where we may feel stuck or like nothing is moving. Thank you for continuing to pour out your spirit. Thank you for reminding me of your promises you have for me. Thank you for continuously being faithful and good to us, even when we aren't faithful. In Jesus' mighty name, amen.

Day 11

Change Your Tune

"Sing to him a new song; play skillfully, and shout for joy."

- Psalm 33:3, NIV

On occasions, I murmured and complained while waiting for my kingdom marriage. I laughed at myself, and I'm sure God laughed with me. I'm sure He said, "If you just will be patient my daughter." Instead of murmuring about why it hasn't happened or when it is going to happen, begin to give thanks to God. Thank God for preparing both your hearts and minds. Thank God for detouring you both from harm, seen and unseen. Give God praise and worship God for who He is. Sing to Him a new song!

Change your tune. Sing something to Him that's new. Sometimes we get on the merry-go-round. Instead, we must put our trust in the Lord. We must trust in God despite what we see. We must praise Him in advance for what He is doing. Let your worship declare the goodness of God in every season. We sometimes become frustrated because we want things to happen in our way and in our time. God doesn't work on our schedule. Yet, He is continually worthy of being worshipped.

now

Through worship, declare an atmosphere shift.

Activation

Listen to worship music and praise God.

Reflect

What has your attitude and feelings been in the wait?

_____

_____

_____

_____

What have you been talking with God about regarding your kingdom marriage promise?

_____

_____

_____

_____

How has worship transformed your outlook on your kingdom marriage promise? What changes will you make?

_____

_____

_____

_____

Pray

Father God, I praise you now and in advance for what you are doing. I thank you for my kingdom marriage promise. I repent for complaining or murmuring. Your timing is never off. Thank you that I'm changing my tune and deciding to worship you. Despite how I may feel or what I see, I choose to praise you. Thank you for redirecting my steps and keeping me from harm, seen and unseen. Thank you for transforming my heart and mind in the process. I will continue to give you glory and honor as I wait. In Jesus' mighty name, amen.

Day 18

yes and Amen

"For no matter how many promises God has made, they are "Yes" in Christ. And so through him the "Amen" is spoken by us to the glory of God."

- 2 Corinthians 1:20, NIV

At times in my life, I felt like God did for others, but not much for me. God agreed to my kingdom marriage promise. He was waiting for me to concur and say, "Amen." Before the foundation of this world, God spoke about everything in my life. God was healing me from the negative thoughts I had about myself. He called me to be a wife. God showed me in a dream that I was getting married. I was in a room getting ready and putting on my makeup. Afterwards, I kept having similar dreams and was reminded by God that my kingdom marriage was coming up. He wanted me to see a glimpse of what's ahead so that I would be prepared. I received confirmation several times. I couldn't keep up with the confirmations and write them all. Be encouraged. God said, "Yes." No matter what your current situation looks like, if you don't have any potential candidates to date, you have been single for years, or you feel like you aren't good enough for this blessing, soon your kingdom marriage will display God's glory and purpose on Earth. Your marriage will bless many others. God will get the glory from everything you have been through and in your obedience to Him.

now

His promises are yes and amen!

Activation

Listen to "Promises" by Maverick City Music online.

Reflect

What promises has God approved of regarding your kingdom marriage promise?

_____

_____

_____

_____

In what ways have you come into agreement (amen) with your kingdom marriage promise?

_____

_____

_____

_____

What ways has the enemy tried to block or hinder your kingdom marriage promise?

_____

_____

_____

_____

How has God equipped you to continue to believe in your kingdom marriage promise?

_____

_____

_____

_____

Pray

Father God, thank you that your promises are *yes* and *amen*. Thank you that my kingdom marriage promise is yes and amen. Thank you that your word shall go forth and do what it was sent to accomplish. Thank you that none of your promises shall be withheld in my life. Thank you for connecting me to my kingdom spouse. Thank you for removing the barriers and we would continue to follow your will. Thank you for the wise Godly counselors you have surrounded me with. Thank you for seeing and meeting my every need. Thank you for reminding me about your faithfulness. My faith will continue to increase in you. Thank you that in due season, it will be here at the appointed time. In Jesus' mighty name, amen.

Day 19

get out of god's Way

"For my thoughts are not your thoughts, neither are your ways my ways," declares the LORD. As the heavens are higher than the earth, so are my ways higher than your ways and my thoughts than your thoughts."

- Isaiah 55:8, NIV

As a young woman, I was used to doing things how I saw fit. I didn't consider asking God if I should date a specific person. I didn't include God in what I was doing in my relationships. I was following my flesh more than the Holy Spirit. At times, I knew better, but didn't act better. I wonder how much heartbreak I could have saved myself if I had simply asked God. In my early 20's, I started to seek God more in everything. I asked God what I should do when it came to people entering my life. I sought God and waited for His answer instead of going with what I wanted or felt at the moment. As God was revealing to me more about my kingdom marriage, I started following my old patterns. I still thought about how it would happen. I became frustrated when trying to figure out only what

God knew. I fully surrendered and realized that it wasn't going to happen in my way.

Your kingdom marriage is going to happen how God designed it to happen. He is God! It doesn't matter if it doesn't make sense to you. He wants to do it in His way, plan, and time. We sometimes become upset and pout to God when it's not moving fast enough or not happening how we thought it would happen. Surrender those thoughts and ways to God. He knows best. Out of fear and doubt, we can try to control things. We may think that if it doesn't happen when and how we want, the whole thing could be ruined. We may believe that we might miss out or someone could take our future spouse away and have other irrational fears. We must surrender those thoughts, fears, and insecurities. The enemy wants us to be so consumed in fear and doubt that we walk away from the promise. "Well God, he's taking too long, he's not paying attention to me, maybe this really isn't the one for me because he's acting this way," may be some of your thoughts. We can get frustrated enough that we walk away, because it's not happening how we want it to happen.

God wants you to rest in Him and allow Him to steer the way, not the other way around. Trust in God even when it is not making sense. He knows the details. His ways are higher than ours. Allow God to do what He does so that He can surprise you.

now

Get your hands off the steering wheel and give it to God!

Activation

Say this aloud: Father God, I release control over my kingdom marriage to you. I will get out of your way and let you put it together in your time. Forgive me for the times I have gotten in your way. I repent for actions that were not aligned to your will. I give you full and complete control over my kingdom marriage. I ask you to move in this area of my life. I will be obedient to your instructions. I give you permission to be God in my life. Thank you for doing what only you can do.

Reflect

In what ways have you gotten in God's way?

_____

_____

_____

_____

In what ways have you tried to do things in your own strength instead of waiting on God for His divine plan?

_____

_____

_____

_____

What do you need to fully surrender to the Lord in this area?

_____

_____

_____

_____

What patterns of thought or behavior did you have or currently have that God wants to break?

_____

_____

_____

_____

Pray

Father God, thank you for keeping your promises to me. I will get out of your way and allow you to be God in my life. Teach me how to rest in you even when I don't understand everything. Help me to trust you even when it seems like nothing is moving. Continue to connect my future husband and I together and order our steps. Thank you for moving in my life and in his life. Thank you for making our crooked places straight. Thank you for trusting me with what you have already given. Continue to strengthen the areas where I'm weak. Continue to help me not to get weary in well doing but know that in due season I will reap if I faint not. In Jesus' mighty name, amen.

Day 20

Tug of War in Faith

"Now faith is the substance of things hoped for, the evidence of things not seen."

- Hebrews 11:1, NKJV

Many times, in my life I felt as if I was in a tug of war. The enemy knew what I could get upset about and emotionally struggle. I became doubtful. I wasn't fully surrendering my kingdom marriage over to God. I expected God to tell me something. When I prayed about it, the enemy came with his schemes.

The enemy may try to sow in us false dreams, doubt, fear, or confusion. We must stand on the Word of God and know that by faith we are shielded. Sometimes we may feel we are being pulled from one side to another. Despite what we see and how our circumstance appears, we must continue to hope and not waiver in our faith. When we don't see anything happening around us, faith is what we stand on. Our faith is now! It will be the very foundation of our kingdom marriage. Our faith is what is going to pull us through, not just in the beginning. It will help to anchor us when things start to get a little stormy and when inevitable tests come to shake our marriage.

If you feel battle fatigue while you are praying and fasting for your kingdom marriage, don't give up. Continue to put on the armor of God. We are victorious through Jesus. We must take authority over demonic influence that is trying to steal, kill, and destroy our promise. Don't allow the enemy to cause you to worry, be doubtful, anxious, or fearful of the unknown. Trust what God told and shown you. Believe that He is going to complete what He started in you. Ask God to pull the territory away from the enemy and release His blessings. When in doubt, trust God.

now

Activate your faith.

Activation

Examine the tug of war you're in with your faith.

Reflect

How much territory has the enemy gained in your tug of war? Have you given him any leverage through your words and actions?

_____

_____

_____

_____

Where is God in this tug of war? What is He doing?

_____

_____

_____

_____

What do you need to do to keep your position of faith?

_____

_____

_____

_____

Pray

Father God, thank you for holding on to me during this tug of war. Thank you for not leaving me or forsaking me. Thank you for not allowing the enemy to overtake me in this process. I repent for giving the enemy legal access to mess with me. I renounce word curses I have spoken. I will continue to speak life over my future kingdom marriage promise. I will continue to have faith despite what is going on around me. I will choose to believe in the goodness of who you are. Thank you for keeping me. Thank you for increasing my faith in you. Thank you for canceling the assignment of the enemy off my kingdom marriage promise. In Jesus' mighty name, amen.

Day 21

Rise and Pray

"Why are you sleeping?" He asked them. "Get up and pray so that you will not fall into temptation."

- Luke 22:46

As I was delighting in the Lord, God showed me what to pray for concerning my future spouse. The Lord stopped me and told me to pray while going about my everyday activities. "Right now, God?" I asked. He instructed me what to pray about. One time, God told me that my future spouse was facing a lot of anxiety and fear. I started praying for him and speaking the word. We must pray, intercede, and seek God as instructed by Him. I keep written prayers for my future spouse in a document. I continue to record prayers for his purity, family, purpose, mental and emotional health, etc.

God is calling us to pray for our future spouse to intercede for them. We may not be sure of who they are or what's going on with them, but God hears our prayers. I believe prayers change things in the spiritual realm. What a beautiful thing it is to pray for our future spouse, whether we met them or not. We must rise, pray, and be obedient to the Lord's prompting. Sometimes God places an impression to immediately pray, wherever we are. Not tomorrow, not next week, next month, but right then! We don't know what is on the other side of our obedience. Continue to pray and don't get weary in well doing. Sometimes, the manifestation of the prayer may not be on our timetable. Keep praying!

now

Pray without ceasing.

Activation

Pray and ask God what areas He is asking you to pray for about your future husband. Write the specific prayers.

Reflect

How is your prayer life? What have you been praying for?

_____

_____

_____

_____

What are some things that you are praying about to prepare yourself for your kingdom marriage?

_____

_____

_____

_____

What is God directing you to pray for regarding your future husband?

_____

_____

_____

_____

Pray

Father God, I come to you with thanksgiving for what you are doing in and through me. Thank you for impressing on my heart and transferring to my spirit what to pray for. Thank you for what you are doing in my future husband's life. Thank you for preparing and working in him. Thank you that strongholds are being broken right now. Thank you that everything that tries to come into his mind is broken. Every high thing that tries to exalt itself against the knowledge of God, I cast it down right now. Thank you for building up my spirit and to know the difference between your voice and the enemy. Thank you for restoring me and him. I speak life over my kingdom marriage. I command every plot from the enemy to cease now in the name of Jesus. Every temptation that comes to his mind that tries to steer him off course, I bind that spirit now and loosen your Holy Spirit. Remind him that when he is weak, you are strong. I cancel the assignment now and I'm not moving away from my position of faith. Thank you God that my faith is causing breakthrough and deliverance. God, help me to stay in prayer despite what I may see or feel. In Jesus' mighty name, amen.

Day 22

Kairos

"The Lord is not slow in keeping his promise, as some understand slowness. Instead he is patient with you, not wanting anyone to perish, but everyone to come to repentance."

- 2 Peter 3:9, NIV

I learned to let go of the need for control, which was scary. Holding on to the need for control meant I could get less hurt from people, and I would be so busy that I didn't have to think about or feel loneliness. I thought I could have more control over what happened to me.

Many times, we think we are in control, but we aren't. It seems as if the need to control was a protective mechanism. I guarded myself even from people who wanted to genuinely be a part of my life. I had a hard time trusting people's true intentions. I had been so hurt in the past, I was on the lookout for the next person that was going to leave or hurt me. Life will happen, people will hurt us, and disappointments will take place. These things will occur, but the beauty is that God has everything worked out. When it comes to our kingdom marriage promise, it will happen in God's timing. Kairos is God's timing and kronos is man's time. Kairos means the appointed time for the purpose of God. Many times, we want to rush things or move it along because we think God is moving too slow. We are impatient. We must learn to fully surrender the need for control. God isn't going to move any faster. We can't manipulate God or the situation. We must learn to rest in the process. The process is not easy, but it will be worth it. We must let go of the need for control. Once we are married, we are united with our husband. We can't try to dominate the situation. We must learn to submit to one another and walk in accordance with God's will.

now

Relax and trust's God's timing.

Activation

Ask the Lord what season you're in. Seek the Lord's face. Focus on what He wants you to do right now.

Reflect

What season are you currently in with regards to your kingdom marriage promise (single, dating, courting, etc.) Do you feel the Lord has been slow in fulfilling His promise?

_____

_____

_____

_____

What does the Lord desire you to focus on now?

_____

_____

_____

_____

In what ways do you need to surrender control and fully yield to God?

_____

_____

_____

_____

Pray

Father God, thank you that time is in your hands. Thank you that I don't have to rush my kingdom marriage or try to make it happen on my own. Thank you that in your kairos moment, it will happen as you see fit. Thank you for the season and purpose you have in my life right now. Thank you for preparing and purifying me in the waiting process. Thank you for moving the wrong people out and the right people in. Remove connections that aren't from you. I give you permission to be God in my life. I understand I may not get everything you're doing right now, and it's okay. I appreciate you God for being patient with me and when I'm restless or frustrated. Thank you for entrusting me with what you have called me to do now. Thank you that in due season, it will come. Your promises will not be withheld from my life. I thank you for setting everything up at the right place and time. In Jesus' mighty name, amen.

Day 23

Worth the Wait

"Hope deferred makes the heart sick, but a longing fulfilled is a tree of life."

- Proverbs 13:12, NIV

As I entered my master's program I thought, "Maybe I will meet my future husband during this time." I thought the same while I was working on my bachelor's, and that didn't happen. I met a lot of people during my undergraduate years at school. Some friends I still have now. I have been single for two years and not dating. Some men have shown interest in me, but it didn't grow into anything bigger. Some of my friends are getting married and starting their families. I knew I wasn't getting married anytime soon but was hoping I would at least be building a committed relationship during this season. It's not taking place. I've learned that there is a time and season for everything and not compare my journey to someone else's. My longing to be married is a part of God's desire and will for my life. I began to struggle in my faith. At times I got so frustrated I didn't want to be bothered with men at all. I just wanted to stay focused on the task at hand, which were the assignments the Lord has given me. Being honest, I felt sad, disappointed, anxious, and agitated. I feared missing out, like I was lagging. I did miss getting dressed up, going on dates, and having a boyfriend.

I knew the Lord was doing a new thing, and it's okay for me to be by myself in this season. Sometimes, I felt like my kingdom marriage wouldn't come. I was stuck in doubt and disappointment and my vision was cloudy. Hope deferred was making my heart sick and I needed the Lord to uplift me. I was codependent in relationships and heavily relied on validation from people. The Lord wanted to remove my overreliance on others so that I could rely on Him.

No matter what your situation looks like, keep the faith. Whether it's waiting for your kingdom spouse to approach you, believing who God said is your husband, going through rough patches, and believing that the promise still stands, your promise is still here. You may have gone through heartbreaks and disappointments, but the longing for your kingdom marriage will be fulfilled by God, in His time and His way. Trust God in the middle, no matter how long you have been waiting. God isn't finished with you.

now

Don't let the wait become a weight.

Activation

Talk with God. Think about what ways you haven't fully surrendered to the Lord.

Reflect

In what ways has your hope been deferred in this season?

_____

_____

_____

_____

_____

_____

_____

What losses, disappointments, and hurts have you dealt with or are currency dealing with?

_____

_____

_____

_____

In what ways, if any, have you allowed the wait to become a weight?

_____

_____

_____

_____

In what ways are you releasing your concerns to God in this season? How is He giving you rest?

_____

_____

_____

_____

Pray

Father God, thank you for removing any fear or anxiety from me. Thank you for removing false burdens or responsibilities I have been carrying. I surrender fully to you, and I understand you will give me rest. Thank you that the wait for this kingdom marriage promise will not become a weight. Thank you for covering me and my future spouse from the tactics of the enemy. Thank you for continuing to walk with me during this process. Replenish my hope in this season that I may not become weary or forfeit your promise. Despite what I see, I will continue to have faith. Thank you for turning around every hurt, loss, and disappointment. I know it will all work out for my good. Thank you for continuing to move on my behalf. Thank you for giving me rest in this season when I feel heavy. In Jesus's mighty name, amen.

Day 24

Purpose Over Preference

"Now to him who is able to do immeasurably more than all we ask or imagine, according to his power that is at work within us."

- Ephesians 3:20, NIV

Growing up, I didn't have many preferences when it came to who I would marry. I didn't have a skin tone, height, occupation, or salary requirement. I wanted someone who shared the same beliefs and values I had. I desired a man with integrity and compassion, who was family-oriented, motivated, after God's heart, and would stick by me through thick and thin.

We typically think we know exactly what we need. However, God knows what we want and need. We may be rigid in our preferences and don't want to move away from them. God knows who our husband will be and the areas where he will be complementary to us. Our kingdom spouse will not be perfect, but they will be as God designed. We must give God our preferences so that He can give us our purpose partner. God's ways are not our ways, and neither are His thoughts (Isaiah 55 8:9). I'm not the best chef but I can make some signature dishes. This is not my strongest area. My future husband may compliment me in that area where I lack. In areas where your husband isn't strong, you will be able to help him.

now

Trust what God has for you, not what you
have for yourself.

Activation

If you have a list of preferences that wasn't Holy Spirit led, rip it up. Create a new list with the leading of the Holy Spirit, with the purposes and qualities of your future spouse.

Reflect

What preferences do you have? Do these preferences match up with God's purpose for your life?

_____

_____

_____

_____

What are some values that you want your future husband
to share with you?

_____

_____

_____

_____

What areas will your future husband be complementary
in and vice versa?

_____

_____

_____

_____

What will be the purpose of your union together?

_____

_____

_____

_____

Pray

Father God, Thank you for the love and grace you show me. Thank you that you're God in my life so that I don't have to be. Thank you for ordering my footsteps in the right direction and knowing what is best for me. Thank you that you're going to use all things for my good. I thank you that you see my heart's desires and you desire to exceed them. As I get in alignment with your will, I will see your purpose in what you're doing in every season. Thank you for not letting me settle. Thank you for allowing me to be purpose-driven and discovered by my future spouse. I'm believing that amazing things are going to happen in my marriage because I will be keeping you during it. In Jesus' mighty name I pray, amen.

Day 25

Now You're Speaking My Language

"Let all that you do be done in love."

- 1 Corinthians 16:14, ESV

In one of my psychology courses, I was required to take the love languages assessment based on Gary Chapman's book. My love languages in order: quality time, words of affirmation, physical touch, acts of service, and gifts. I wasn't surprised because I appreciate quality time. I keep a list in one of my journals of activities I hope to do with my future husband. Later, words of affirmation may become my number one because of its importance. I love to receive cards, compliments, and encouragement. I keep cards and I save certain meaningful messages. I love to give words of affirmation. I plan on hiding notes of encouragement for my future husband to find.

We have different ways about how we receive and give love. It is vital to know how you receive love and how to give love to your future husband. Love languages can change over time. Let all you do be done in love! We must carefully watch our words and behaviors and make sure that our actions are in love. Theorist Robert Sternburg created a theory and named it the triangular theory of love. He discussed three components, including intimacy, passion, and commitment. Intimacy is the sharing of personal thoughts and emotions, passion is the physical attraction, and commitment is standing by one another and moving toward a shared purpose (Sternberg, 1986). What kind of love do you want to give and receive in your kingdom marriage?

now

Everyone gives and receives love differently.

Activation

Go to the following website: www.5lovelanguages.com and complete the love language quiz under the romantic session. View the results.

Reflect

What are your top five love languages? List examples for each love language you want to receive.

_____

_____

_____

_____

If you know your future husband's love languages, list them here? Write out ways to express each love language to him. If you don't know, add examples for each love language.

_____

_____

_____

_____

_____

_____

_____

_____

_____

_____

In past relationships, did you receive love the way you desired? Why or why not?

_____

_____

_____

_____

In past relationships, did you give love the way you desired? Why or why not?

_____

_____

_____

_____

Pray

Father God, thank you for the love you have graciously shown me. Thank you for expressing your love to me in different ways. I pray over my future husband and ask you to remove heartbreaks and disappointments. Give him a heart of flesh, purify, and renew the right spirit in him. I pray that he is willing and open to receiving your love and love through me. I pray that any walls that have been built are removed. I pray over his soul (mind, will, and emotions). I pray that we will connect as you see fit. I pray that we will show Christ's love through us. I pray that we will reflect your love and that it overflows into the hearts of many. I pray that when things get rough, we will turn to you and seek you for the answer. I pray that any hindrances and barriers that may be preventing us from meeting or moving forward are removed. I thank you God that my future marriage shall be blessed. In Jesus' mighty name, amen.

Day 26

Love in Action

"Love is patient, love is kind. It does not envy, it does not boast, it is not proud. It does not dishonor others, it is not self-seeking, it is not easily angered, it keeps no record of wrongs. Love does not delight in evil but rejoices with the truth. It always protects, always trusts, always hopes, always perseveres."

- 1 Corinthians 13:4-8, NIV

I want to pour out love to people. We know love as a feeling and display it through our actions. I could have loved more. I could have been more patient and not kept score of the wrongs people have done to me. It can be easy for us to not act loving, especially when someone catches us on a bad day. Sometimes we feel that to give love, we must first receive love. This will be important as you enter your kingdom marriage. You may become inpatient with your husband. You may have to wait before you speak so that you don't say something offensive. You might boast about what you do for them. You may not think you are the one with an issue and the other is to blame. Sometimes, there will be incidents when you will have to ask the Lord to help you let go. It's like building a wall. Refuse to build with bricks of pride, offense, bitterness, and unforgiveness to create a wall of separation between you and your spouse. Love is protecting, trusting, and persevering. Your commitment will be tested by the trials in your marriage. We can't predict what is going to happen in the future. At times, we must make sacrifices that are not easy. God is a true representation of love. We must continue to walk in love as Christ desires us to.

now

Love in your actions, despite the trials.

Activation

Ask God what challenges may arise. Ask how He is preparing you to love and grow in that way (according to the above Scripture).

Reflect

In what ways does God show His love to you?

_____

_____

_____

_____

Do you struggle with any of the phrases in the Scripture (e.g., not being patient, etc.)?

_____

_____

_____

_____

In what ways has God challenged and told you the changes He wants to make in you?

_____

_____

_____

_____

What does 1 Corinthians 13:4-8 mean to you?

_____

_____

_____

_____

In what ways will you show your future husband love-in-action? What are some of the sacrifices you will make?

_____

_____

_____

_____

Pray

Father God, thank you for showing me your love. Thank you for changing me to be able to love more like you. Thank you for my kingdom spouse and that you are healing and transforming him. Help me to see the changes I need to make to be able to give love in action. Help me to make necessary sacrifices. When the time is here, help me to be patient with my spouse. Help me not be easily offended or prideful. Thank you for your overflowing love. May my love overflow to my future husband. May I turn to you when it becomes difficult. Give me guidance to make the right decisions and to be led by your Holy Spirit. Thank you that our love and trust in you will be a solid foundation for our marriage. Thank you for already making the crooked paths straight. I praise you even now for what you have done and will continue to do. In Jesus' mighty name, amen.

Day 21

fill Me Up

"May the God of hope fill you with all joy and peace as you trust in Him, so that you may overflow with hope by the power of the Holy Spirit."

- Romans 15:13, NIV

I've asked God to fill me again. One night, I had a heavenly visitation from God. Afterward, I physically felt the presence of God and had an indescribable peace, joy, and bliss. I don't have the words to justify what the presence of God feels like. I woke up and His presence lingered around me. I didn't want to go back to sleep. I knew I was feeling the Holy Spirit around and on me.

I was still posting encouragement videos on a popular social media site. Many of us have lost our hope, joy, or peace in the journey of waiting on the Lord for our promise. We may have been hurt by people, experienced disappointments, felt lost or lonely. Hold on, God is getting ready to fill you up with His love, joy, and peace. He is a God of more than enough and is pursuing your every need. Through the Holy Spirit, we can hear, understand, and receive comfort from God. You may not know how much longer you must wait for God to bring your spouse. It's okay. You may not know who your spouse is or from where he will come. It's okay. You may not know what changes or sacrifices must be made. It's okay. The God of hope will fill you with His peace and joy as you continue to trust in Him. You will feel indescribable tranquility as you continue to walk and talk with God. To some, the joy and peace you have may not make sense. The Lord's presence will come over you during it all. You may be filled with the Holy spirit, but sometimes we need a refresh and to be filled again. As you approach your kingdom marriage, you will feel God's peace overflow in your life. The more you hope and trust in God in this promise, the more you will feel His power working in your life.

now

God is getting ready to fill you until you overflow.

Activation

Ask God to fill you in whatever area you're lacking.

Ask Him to meet your physical, emotional, financial, and spiritual needs.

Reflect

Are you having a hard time trusting in God in this season?

_____

_____

_____

_____

What has God been telling you? What are some things He revealed to you?

_____

_____

_____

_____

What areas is God going to fill or refill as you continue to trust in Him?

_____

_____

Pray

Father God, thank you for filling me up with your Holy Spirit. Thank you for filling my empty areas. Thank you for fulfilling my every longing and desire. Thank you for filling me with your peace, love, and joy. Thank you for giving me clarity, understanding, and wisdom when I need help. Continue to guide me and my future spouse. Continue to fill us with the fruits of the spirit. Continue to fill our hearts and minds with your Word. May we know to rest in you and not worry. May we get what we need to learn in this season so that we can pass the test. Thank you for being God in our lives. In Jesus' mighty name, amen.

Day 28

Faith Over Fear

"She is clothed with strength and dignity, and she laughs without fear of the future."

- Proverbs 31:25, NLT

Having faith in any area of our lives can be hard. It was difficult for me to have faith in the process. I like to know the plan. Not knowing details and not seeing what God was doing, was frustrating. I knew that some of the details He showed me were for an appointed time. Even then, it was hard for me to be patient while waiting for those events to manifest. God had to work on my level of patience. When He showed me things, mainly through dreams and visions, I got excited. Just because He showed me didn't mean that it was time for those things to take place.

Some of you may have experienced God speaking to you about things related to your kingdom marriage. Many times, we must have faith, despite how long it takes. For others, it may be right around the corner, or it may take years. This isn't necessarily a bad thing. We must not want the right thing at the wrong time. We must be patient enough to allow God to connect all the pieces. God sometimes shows us a few pieces, not the whole puzzle.

The enemy tried to attack me in the waiting process by using fear. I had a lot of fears, and God was working on me. I talked with God about each fear, and He helped me to see what was going on. God, being my counselor, was counseling me as I brought each fear to Him. As I was taking each thought captive, He was making it clear. The Proverbs 31 woman knew who she was in God, her confidence was in Him. She didn't fear the days to come because she knew the God she served.

Many of us are walking and talking as if God isn't going to come through. We may have frightening moments, but we must get back into the face of God. We must not move from our position of faith. Stay encouraged because God will always come through. Your kingdom marriage is coming, but in His timing.

now

Don't allow the enemy to consume you with fear, stand in your position of faith.

Activation

List the fears you have pertaining to your kingdom marriage promise. Discuss your fears with God.

Reflect

What fears did you and God discuss?

_____

_____

_____

_____

What is the root of your fears?

_____

_____

_____

_____

How is God delivering you from your fears?

_____

_____

_____

_____

In what ways are you willing to move in faith with God?

_____

_____

_____

_____

Pray

Father God, I come to you in faith. I understand it is impossible to please you without faith. Thank you for removing fears before my kingdom marriage. Thank you for setting me free from everything that is trying to hold me back. Thank you for developing my character into a Proverbs 31 woman. Thank you for clothing me with strength and dignity. Thank you for continuing to walk with me on this journey. Help me to have faith instead of fear, despite what I can't see. Help me to patiently wait with faith and grace. Remove fear from my future husband's thoughts. I pray that he walks in faith knowing you are connecting both of us together. Continue to strengthen me as I walk. Help me to not get weary in well doing. I thank you for breaking the spirit of fear. I praise you and I give you the honor and glory. In Jesus' name, amen.

Day 29

Dancing Shoes

"You have turned my mourning into joyful dancing. You have taken away my clothes of mourning and clothed me with joy."

- Psalm 30:11, NLT

I love to dance and look forward to doing so with my future spouse. No matter what kind of mood I'm in, when I play music, I start dancing. I then feel better. For many people, dancing is a celebratory act. We often see dancing at major events including weddings. Depending on the tempo of the music, we may dance slow or fast. I'm not good at walking in heels, especially when dancing. It's easier to dance without heels. I don't want to be limited in any way.

God is taking away your mourning clothes and replacing it with clothing of joy. How awesome is this? Step into the fresh joy the Lord has made. You will dance through different seasons of life with your future husband, the ups and downs. Keep dancing. God is dancing with you during seasons when you feel alone. You may feel like you don't have anyone to celebrate moments with, but God is always with you. It's time to celebrate what God is doing before your kingdom marriage. It's time to get on your dancing shoes!

now

Dance through the storms of life.

Activation

Put on some music and dance!

Reflect

What have you been mourning about lately? What are you using to help you through this season?

_____

_____

_____

_____

How is dancing beneficial to you?

_____

_____

_____

_____

What life storms do you think you will be dancing through
with your kingdom spouse?

_____

_____

_____

_____

Pray

Father God, thank you for giving me fresh joy. Thank you that what I have sown in tears, I will reap in joy! Thank you that my kingdom marriage promise is coming at your perfect timing. I will put on my dancing shoes in the meantime and celebrate. I praise you for what I'm going through. I will continue to dance through whatever storm I face. I choose to celebrate what you're doing in my life. I choose to have joy during my wait. I choose to get up and dance. I will activate my faith in this season. I will continue to believe in what you have shown me. I won't let the enemy steal my joy. I will continue to praise you even when I don't understand. I thank you for walking with me in every season. I thank you for connecting the dots and removing the barriers. I give you all the honor and glory. In Jesus' mighty name, amen.

Full Circle

"Being confident of this, that he who began a good work in you will carry it on to completion until the day of Christ Jesus."

- Philippians 1:6, NIV

While preparing for my kingdom marriage promise, God led me to create a prophetic diary. I include specific prophetic dreams, notes, confirmations, etc. in my diary. I mainly keep it to document and date my dreams and visions. I ask the Lord for what He wants me to understand or directive He wants to give. Normally, God confirms and reconfirms and shares with me little secrets from Heaven. Sometimes, God will show me something just to soothe a doubt. Often, He confirms it through a visual message. Then, I went to God's written word. God showed me glimpses of what was to come. When I didn't understand, I was able to make sense of it later. God has shown me and my future spouse dancing, singing, talking, etc. Sometimes, when you don't pay attention, God will keep showing you. That's what He did with me. I wasn't paying it much attention or fully praying about it. When I started to pray about it, I understood what God was doing. God speaks in many ways, sometimes it may be a vision, dream, Scripture, or another way. God is always speaking.

God revealed to me in dreams and visions some of the things to come in my kingdom marriage. He showed a glimpse of a song or event. I didn't have the whole picture, just a piece of the puzzle. God connected the dreams and visions and added on to them. Sometimes, when I didn't understand it, I pressed into what the Holy Spirit was saying. Over time, my dreams, visions, and events started to come full circle. I began to understand after prayer and seeking God's heart. I wondered why God showed me some of the things if it wasn't going to soon happen. I knew God would laugh at me in Heaven. I wanted God to show me and prepare me, but I also didn't want to know. I've asked God to surprise me! God is the best gift and blessing giver.

You may have received prophetic words, dreams, or visions. Hold on, write, and date them. Add as God continues to speak to you. God wants your kingdom marriage for you. He may show some pieces of the puzzle, but not the whole puzzle. He wants you to seek and trust in Him for the rest.

now

It's all coming together full circle.

Activation

Keep a list or journal of what the Lord speaks to you
pertaining to your kingdom marriage promise. Add
the date He showed you and then date it when
you see it come to pass.

Reflect

What are some revelations that God has given you?

_____

_____

_____

_____

What pieces of the puzzle are missing?

_____

_____

_____

_____

How has your confidence been in the Lord in this season when you don't feel like you have all the information?

_____

_____

_____

_____

How is the Lord increasing your trust in Him as you wait?

_____

_____

_____

_____

Pray

Father God, thank you for revealing to me what I need to know before my kingdom marriage. Thank you for moving all the pieces of the puzzle together. Thank you for trusting me enough to show me so that I know how to pray and prepare. Thank you for removing doubt. Help me to surrender control and let go of the things that are trying to hold my faith captive. Help me to patiently wait and not go ahead of you. Help me to trust what you are showing to me in the spiritual realm despite what I see around me. I pray over my future husband and that you continue to lead and guide him. I pray that you continue to connect him to the right places. I ask that you help build his faith when he feels confused or uncertain. I ask that your peace would overflow in our lives, and we may learn to continue to lean on you for everything. I pray that we continue to follow your will and to rest in you. In Jesus' mighty name, amen.

Closing Prayer

Father God, thank you for giving me this assignment and bringing it to completion. I pray that this helps each person that it is intended to help. I thank you that you heard the prayers of those reading. Thank you that through this process they are drawing close to you. In the mist of their misunderstanding or heartbreak, you are drawing close to them. I pray that you continue to increase the fruits of the spirits in their lives. Thank you that in due season, their kingdom marriage will be here. I thank you God for strengthening those that feel weary in the wait. Continue to give them encouragement to weather the wait and to go through the process. In Jesus' mighty name, I pray, amen.

Closing Encouragement

I want to thank everyone that has purchased this devotional journal (vol. 2). Thank you for those that have shared an exclusive encouragement. Continue to stand on what God has told you, no matter what you see. Continue to believe that the Lord will fulfill His promises to you. I believe in each one of you. God is going to amaze you beyond whatever you could ask, think, or imagine. I encourage you to patiently wait on the Lord.

Warm Regards,
Janay Wells

Future Mrs.

By Janay Wells

Dear God, you are preparing me to be a bride.

It has been a journey, it has been a bumpy ride

My heart has been broken and I struggled with rejection on the inside

Emotions would flood in like a wave after a wave, low or hide tide

I'm trying to do it right, it's your word in my heart that I would hide

Making a prophetic declaration of who you say I am, you are my guide

The enemy would try to come in, his mission was to divide

You know who I am, now I have to measure up and decide

It is your Holy spirit in my heart to come in and reside.

You're always making a way, Jehovah Jireh to provide

My soul is becoming whole, I have to heal

The enemy's mission is to come and steal

Crush the head of the enemy, like Eve did with her heel

Tired of the imperfections I have to conceal

Trust the process, I can't always go by how I feel

It's my faith that keeps me when I kneel

Preparation is a journey, I'm trying to keep it real

Knowing that I'm developing, it may not be ideal

I still believe in what God said, he made a seal

Sometimes, I'm like Jesus take the wheel

Trials and tests come, I'm trying not to lose my zeal

The Lord says hold tight, here comes the reveal

Exclusive Encouragement

By Janelle Cumberbatch
(Confess & Be Healed Ministries)

As you navigate your day-to-day life waiting for the promise of marriage to be fulfilled in your life, know, and understand that marriage is and has always been, a good thing. It was created as a gift from our Father, intended to help us navigate life here on earth, and keep from sin. As you faithfully pray, fast, and seek our Father, know that you are waiting on a good thing and remain steadfast in doing so. Understand that it is our Father's desire to gift us with a Godly union that glorifies Him. He knows and understands how to give us good Gifts and is the creator of all good things. Matthew 7:11 says "though you are evil, know how to give good gifts to your children, how much more will your Father in heaven give good gifts to those who ask him!" Seasons of waiting are meant to strengthen and prepare you for the many good things that lie ahead, things that you presently could not fathom.

One of my favorite scriptures is Galatians 6:9 which says, "Let us not become weary in doing good, for at the proper time we will reap a harvest if we do not give up."

Be encouraged, knowing that although there may be rough days and seasons where you feel as though marriage is nowhere in sight, the Lord promises us that we will reap, as long as we don't give up. Do not get weary in doing the things you are called to do in your seasons of healing, preparation, and transition. Embrace them as gifts from the Father and allow Him to lead you in all things. If you have been praying, fasting, and waiting on a Godly union, as it aligns with the perfect will of God for your life, it will be given to you. Trust the Lord fully and know that all He prepares for you is good! In time, the Lord wishes to bless all of those who wait upon Him and diligently seek Him first with even more than can be imagined.

Exclusive Encouragement

By Nadesha McPherson
Fuel Your Soul (on YouTube)

When we ask the Lord to choose our spouse, we are handing over control and trusting that He has our best interest in hand. God wants to remind the world what a marriage ordained by Him looks like. He is indeed our perfect match maker.

This journey is definitely not an easy one. It's filled with worries, doubts, and the struggle to trust in God's timing. I believe God wants us to love the way He loves unconditionally. He's teaching us forgiveness, faith and trust for the revelation awaits an appointed time. It speaks of the end and will not prove false. Though it linger, wait for it, it will certainly come and will not delay (Habakkuk 2:3).

Exclusive Encouragement

Kingdom Influencer with Jessica Dos Santos

The waiting season, hahaha. A season that is never constant when it comes to my emotions and how well I wait. Some days are really good and some days are bad, some days I understand God's plan and other days it's like I never received anything from God concerning Kingdom Marriage. But as I wait, it's a time of refinement and a time of me evolving into the woman that God has destined me to be.

It's a time of me breaking mindsets, a time of God introducing me to who He has destined me to be and going through the process of accepting it and walking the path that He has chosen for me.

The wait has different sides for me and has taught me different things, but as I write this, the wait right now has been about rejecting the things that evil altars have spoken over my life, generational holds that have had me going in a path that isn't the one God has for me and accepting my true identity as a daughter of God. It has been a time of me raising an altar for God, honoring Him, offering sacrifices for who He is, what He has done and what He has gotten me through. As the altar has been raised, a shift has taken place, a shift in me from my old self to my new self. The shift brought perspective, a perspective that was in plain sight but never accessible because of mindsets I allowed to grow roots in me and I thought it was a correct mindset.

The wait in itself is like a trip with different destinations and at each destination you experience the newness of that destination and the culture shock of that place and culture, some adaptable and others very hard because it's just foreign, but at everything destination, in every place, within every culture there is what you need for your final destination. It doesn't matter if you are experiencing the ups of the wait or the downs, where you are is needed for where you are going and the blessing of Kingdom Marriage. The preparation is intense because, through the impact it will be huge. Your Kingdom Marriage isn't only a blessing for you, it's a blessing for others and generations to come, it's part of the new that God is doing.

Reference

Sternbery, R. J. (1986). A triangular theory of love. *Psychological Review*, 93, 119-135

About the Author

Janay Wells is a graduate student studying mental health counseling, entrepreneur, author, and executive producer and talk show host of The Janay Wells Show. She dedicates her time to helping others overcome adversities. She is purpose-driven and passionate about sharing her story. She is the Chief Visionary Officer of Janay Cosmetics, a brand that ties together makeup and faith. She hopes to inspire other people to pursue Jesus and to follow their God-given purpose.

Contact

www.janaywells.com

Reach out to share testimonies, book speaking engagements, and more to weatherthewaitdevotional@gmail.com.

Scan For Social Media

Made in the USA
Columbia, SC
07 September 2024

f963d4d6-ed68-4092-bd03-ee2b684d595eR01